TRUE STORIES OF OPEN ADOPTION

Volume One

Edited By
Guylaine Hubbard-Brosmer
and
Ann Wrixon

Text copyright © 2013 Independent Adoption Center
All Rights Reserved
ISBN-13: 978-1494435257
ISBN-10: 149443525X

To Our Children and their Birthparents

To Ed & Angie -
You are an integral part of this big, blended, extended family of ours!
Love,
Guylaine

TRUE STORIES OF OPEN ADOPTION

Acknowledgements

We are grateful to Aki Parker for her expertise and creative eye in designing the cover and photo gallery, as well as for her assistance with formatting the manuscript.

We would also like to thank Robert Sax of SAX PR/Marketing for his professional editorial services.

The following people served as proofreaders:

Jennifer L. Bliss, Psy.D., M.S.W., L.C.S.W.
Britt Cloudsdale, M.S.W.
Delaney Diskin
Alice Hubbell, M.S.W.
Michelle J. Keyes, L.M.S.W.
Elizabeth Kwiatkowski-Wrixon
Sarah Musich, L.C.S.W.
Karen Tirlia, M.S.W.
Kerrin Tomek, M.S.W.
Rebecca Weinberg, M.S.W.
Mallory Winter, L.M.S.W.

The marketing and design expertise of Ryan Schwab and Amalia Gratteri is also greatly appreciated.

TRUE STORIES OF OPEN ADOPTION

Contents

FOREWORD	1
PREFACE	2
HOW OPENNESS CHANGED EVERYTHING	3
MY LIFE IS ALL ABOUT OPEN ADOPTION	7
WE WILL TEACH HIM YOUR NAME	12
FINDING DECLAN'S LITTLE BROTHER	16
THREE WEEKS TO ZOE	27
COMING OUT ON THE OTHER SIDE	30
OVER THE RAINBOW	33
ADOPTIVE MOTHER, BIRTHMOTHER, BEST FRIENDS	37
WHO WILL PICK ME?	39
THREE POINTS OF VIEW	41
OUR LITTLE MIRACLE	46
HOLDING CHLOE FOR THE FIRST TIME	51
NOW THAT OUR CHILDREN ARE GROWN	61
GLOSSARY	63
ABOUT THE EDITORS	65
PHOTO GALLERY	66

Foreword

Bruce Rappaport, Ph.D. founded the Independent Adoption Center in 1982, when "open" adoption was considered a radical concept. Historically, secrecy had defined "closed" adoption; birthmothers and adoptive parents never met and adoption agency workers decided on the placement of the children. The idea of an adoption agency that allowed birthparents to select their child's adoptive parents, meet them prior to the birth, and potentially build a long-term relationship was groundbreaking.

Based on his personal experience of infertility, as well as running an infertility clinic, Dr. Rappaport felt that open adoption would be beneficial for the adoptive parents, the birthparents, and, most importantly, the child. In the more than 30 years since, open adoption has made significant advances into the worlds of private and county adoption.

Adoption experts now agree that open adoption is the better practice. Research shows that it has the best outcomes for adoptees, birthparents and adoptive parents. Open adoption agreements are now legally enforceable in more than 20 states.

Dr. Rappaport retired in 2006 and passed away shortly thereafter. By that time, the IAC had expanded to four states. The IAC board of directors hired Ann Wrixon, M.S.W., M.B.A., to succeed Dr. Rappaport. Under her leadership, the organization expanded further. IAC operates licensed agencies in eight states: California, Connecticut, Florida, Georgia, Indiana, New York, North Carolina, and Texas.

Today, more and more people want to know how open adoption works, and about the challenges adoptive and birth families face as they navigate the process. This book is for them.

True Stories of Open Adoption collects the words and experiences of IAC clients and staff members. It includes stories from adoptive parents, birthparents and siblings, and it highlights the joys and the sorrows that encompass open adoption. We hope that these heartfelt stories will enlighten and inspire all those who are striving to build a family through open adoption.

-- Guylaine Hubbard-Brosmer and Ann Wrixon

Preface

by Kathleen Silber, M.S.W.

When people first hear about open adoption, it often sounds "different" and scary. The potential adopting parents may be afraid of birth family involvement.

What does open adoption mean? How is open adoption different from shared parenting? Will the adoptive parents ever feel that they are the "real" parents? This book answers these and many other questions through poignant true stories that illuminate the world of open adoption.

These families share their experiences of the vicissitudes of adoption, including matches that fell through and other disappointments. The consistent thread through all of the stories is the naturalness of open adoption. Families talk about the loving relationships they establish with the birthparents and the benefits of openness for their children. Readers will see how open adoption works over the years, as some of the adoptees in the book are school-age children or teenagers.

It is our hope that these stories will dispel any fears a reader has about open adoption.

Kathleen Silber is the associate executive director of the Independent Adoption Center. She has more than 40 years of experience working in adoption. In addition, she is the co-author of two classic books on open adoption: "Dear Birthmother" *and* "Children of Open Adoption."

How Openness Changed Everything

by Ann Wrixon – Adoptive Mother & IAC Executive Director

My daughter was only six weeks old when her third foster mother placed her in my arms. She was beautiful, with large brown eyes and thick dark brown hair. My husband and I had been told her mother was stunningly beautiful, and looking at our daughter we believed that must be true.

Her birthmother had voluntarily relinquished her to the California Department of Social Services, but DSS had not made any adoption plan. The county DSS provided us with basic information about our daughter's birthmother, including her height, weight, hair color, and religion.

However, they gave us no medical information. Fortunately my new daughter was healthy, remarkably so. But I quickly found out that having no family medical history meant that every visit to the doctor was an ordeal, frequently resulting in unnecessary and painful tests. I would often weep while holding my screaming daughter as she endured these procedures.

I needed that medical information, so I resolved to find her birth family. During my search, I accidently discovered my daughter's birth name, and was able to quickly locate her original birth certificate with the name of her birthmother. I thought finding her birthmother would be an easy task. Little did I know how arduous and difficult a journey lay ahead.

My search took more than eleven and a half years. I hired eight different private detectives, including one in Europe after I discovered my daughter's birthmother might have emigrated from there. I wrote letters, made phone calls and visited every address that might provide a lead. I also made innumerable online searches, set up a Website, and elicited assistance from many "search angels," volunteers who help individuals search for birth family members.

Time passed and my daughter grew up. She frequently looked in the mirror and wondered from whom she inherited her features. Other times she would ask, "Do you think my birthmother loves me?" I would always nod yes and she would respond, "Then why did she place me for adoption?" This question always made me cry. I wanted to give her the answers she was craving, but no matter how much I loved her, I could not give her the information she so desperately wanted because I did not have it.

I continued to search. I often spent evenings and weekends scouring the Web and continued to consult private detectives. I would lie in bed at night, obsessively going over in my head all the clues I had gathered about where my daughter's birthmother might be. One hunch, in particular, kept recurring. Finally, one night at 2 a.m., I leapt out of bed and rushed to the computer. I checked one more fact, and then it hit me; I knew exactly where she was.

I couldn't sleep and kept watching the clock, willing time to go faster so I could rush to the address where I was certain I would find her. Of course, all sorts of things delayed me the next day. After I dropped my daughter off at a birthday party, I was finally free to pursue my hunch. I drove swiftly to the place where I believed I would finally end my search.

Breathing deeply, I knocked at the door. A woman answered it, and I knew immediately I had finally found her. She was beautiful, perhaps one of the most beautiful people I had ever met. She looked at me quizzically and said, "Yes?"

"Do you have a daughter?" I asked.

My abrupt question didn't seem to surprise her. "Yes, a long time ago," she answered.

"Who you placed for adoption?"

She stepped out of the house and closed the door behind her. "I know who you are," she said. "I have been looking for you, too."

I started to weep. "Do you want to see pictures of your daughter?" I asked. She smiled and nodded. We talked, but I don't remember what I said or how she responded. I could not stop crying and telling her how happy I was to have finally found her.

She was kind to me. We exchanged email addresses and phone

numbers, and agreed to meet again with the daughter we had in common.

Sobbing, I called my husband to tell him the news. Our daughter had a piano recital that afternoon; we agreed to tell her afterwards so she would not be distracted while performing. Driving her to the recital, I struggled to talk about the upcoming performance. It was hard to keep such momentous information from her, even for a couple of hours.

Finally, we returned home and I told her that I had met her birthmother. She started to cry and grabbed me, half-hugging and half-dancing around the living room. "What does she look like?" she asked. I showed her a photo on my phone. She gasped and said, "She is so beautiful." My daughter smiled as she realized that her birthmother was her mirror image. "I want to meet her," she said. I assured her that she would.

Again, events intervened and three months passed before my daughter met her birthmother in person. During that time, I struggled with what this meant for me, for my husband, for our daughter, and for her birthmother. I was relieved that the answers to my daughter's questions were so close, but I was afraid she might be disappointed or hurt.

Surprisingly, the one thing I did not feel was threatened. I was not worried that my place in my daughter's heart would be gone; I knew that was not possible. But I also knew that her heart had always had a place for her birthmother, and that until now it had been achingly empty.

Finally, the day arrived when the three of us were to meet. My daughter was very nervous. We arrived early, and then spent fifteen agonizing minutes waiting for her birthmother to arrive. Finally she drove up, stepped out of the car and approached my daughter, offering her hand to shake. I could tell she was trying not to intrude on anyone's boundaries. Our daughter took her hand and looked into her eyes, and for the first time in her life, she saw another face that resembled her own.

Her birthmother told her she loved her and always had. She told her about her birthfather, and then she told my daughter why she placed her for adoption. I could see my daughter visibly lighten; later she would tell me, "It all makes sense now. She made the right decision. I understand she placed me for adoption because she loved me." I smiled in a way that I had not smiled since the day my daughter's foster mother placed her in my arms.

My daughter's birthmother is a kind, wonderful woman, who has allowed us to be part of her life in ways I never would have dreamed.

She has provided our daughter with the gift of knowing that her adoption was truly done out of love.

This search has transformed all our lives, perhaps mine more than anyone's. The search made me increasingly committed to open adoption and to spreading the message of why it is important. As a result, I switched careers to become the director of the Independent Adoption Center after its founder, Dr. Bruce Rappaport, retired in 2006.

Fortunately, the families at the IAC will never have to seek out the identity of their child's birthparents. They already know who they are because the birthparents choose them to parent their child. Each child will grow up knowing that his or her adoption was done out of love because the adoptive and birthparents will tell them so.

My Life is All About Open Adoption

by Guylaine Hubbard-Brosmer – Adoptive Mother, Birth Grandmother, IAC Adoption Counselor and Research Director

The Adventure Begins

My husband and I had infertility problems, and ultimately I went through surgery and several unsuccessful *in vitro* fertilization attempts. The doctor explained that despite "everything looking perfect," our attempts at achieving a pregnancy would continue to be met with failure.

We joined the local chapter of RESOLVE, a national nonprofit organization focused on infertility and adoption education. It was at one of their public education meetings that we first learned about open adoption.

It was then that we decided to build our family through adoption. We attended more adoption education classes and chose to use an adoption attorney. We worked hard on our single-page "Dear Birthparent" letter. It was the age before digital cameras, so we took several rolls of film to get that one great photo. Once we completed our letter, we mailed out 500 copies, gave another 50 to our attorney, and told everyone we knew that we were trying to adopt.

Over the next several months, we heard about several potential birthparents, and even met a couple of young, pregnant women. We matched with one, only to experience a devastating loss when the baby died just before delivery. We stayed at the hospital with the birthmother for a couple of hours, as she had to endure labor and deliver the stillborn baby.

Not too long after that, we met another teenage girl, along with her mother. The girl was in the process of deciding between us and another couple. After our initial meeting, she wanted to get together again before she made her final decision. She invited us to come to her house, as she had not been feeling well.

We arrived at her house the next morning and her father greeted us. He did not quite know how to tell us that his daughter had delivered the previous night, and that he and his wife were going to help her parent the baby. My husband and I called our attorney, who was flabbergasted that we had "lost" two babies in a very short period.

Finally, we received a phone call from a young woman named Stacey and her boyfriend. Following a long, promising phone conversation, we arranged to meet them in person. Of course, after our two recent disappointments, we were very nervous and did not know what to expect from the meeting.

That initial visit lasted several hours. We met most of Stacey's family and the birthfather. Afterwards, we felt very much like we had known them for a long time. A few days later, our attorney confirmed that this was indeed a match.

We talked to Stacey and her family over the next few weeks and had another visit. We were at the hospital with Stacey's family when she gave birth to our daughter Marielle, thus creating our family. The hospital gave us a room so we could spend as much time as we wanted bonding with our daughter; we also spent some time visiting with Stacey. When Marielle was discharged from the hospital two days later, Mark and I took her home and settled in as a family of three.

A New Addition

We had our first official visit with Marielle's birth family when our daughter was about 10 weeks old. There were plenty of nerves beforehand, but Stacey and her family were always warm and welcoming to us. They made it easy to develop our budding relationship. Stacey and the birthfather were no longer dating after the birth, but Stacey made the effort to include him in the visits. When Stacey later began to date another young man, he also joined us for a visit.

About a month before our daughter's first birthday, Stacey called to tell us that she was pregnant again and still not ready to parent. It took no time at all for us to reply "yes" to adopting again. A few weeks later our son Geremy arrived. Not only were we at the hospital and in the room with Stacey during labor, but I held her hand during the delivery.

Geremy's birthfather had moved out of the area several months earlier, so Stacey's mom and I were her support during and after the delivery. Stacey and I now had a friendship, and we spent much of the time in the hospital together with the new baby.

Stacey and her ex-boyfriend, Marielle's birthfather, were a racially-mixed couple. They had chosen Mark and me, at least in part, because we are a racially-mixed couple too. But life is unpredictable; Geremy's birthfather was Caucasian and this time Stacey delivered a full Caucasian baby into our biracial family. When our children were young, strangers often said to us "Oh how cute, the little girl looks just like mom and the boy looks just like dad." We used those moments as an opportunity to share our open adoption story with others.

My children are now young adults. We have kept in touch over the years with Stacey and have all embraced the fact that we are part of each other's families. We don't live close to each other, so we cherish any opportunities we have to visit. Stacey got married and had three children, so my children have younger siblings. They look up to Marielle and Geremy as their "big brother and sister."

When we get together, we spend time getting caught up on all aspects of our lives – jobs, school, kids' sports and activities, our parents and other family members. We remark on physical and behavioral similarities and differences between the kids, and commiserate because none of them are good at keeping their room clean.

It is inspiring to hear that Stacey has told others that she has no regrets about placing two babies for adoption and that she and her mother promote open adoption. Every time I have thanked her for placing our children with us, she thanks us right back for being great parents. That mutual love and respect is what open adoption is all about.

A New Generation

There is another significant chapter to this story. When my daughter was 18, she found herself pregnant and facing the same choices as her birthmother. It was not an easy process for her or for my husband and me. After nearly 20 years as an adoptive parent and seven years working in the adoption field, I was now experiencing the adoption process as a member of the birth family. We did our best to give Marielle the space and time to come to her own decision.

Our daughter struggled with whether she wanted to parent or place her baby for adoption. As often happens with "young love," she thought that she and her boyfriend would be together forever, so it was natural to attempt to figure out a parenting plan. They jointly made the decisions on placement and the choice of adoptive family, and Marielle's boyfriend was at the hospital for the delivery. Ultimately, however, they did not stay together.

My daughter's birthmother was one of the first people we told about the pregnancy. Although Marielle did not turn to Stacey for advice, she later confided that growing up with a positive open adoption experience made her decision to place the baby a little bit easier.

When Marielle felt more secure in her decision to place, she went through profiles and selected a potential adoptive couple. The couple traveled from Northern California to meet with my daughter and her boyfriend. They had an enjoyable lunch and it seemed like a good match. My daughter was very excited about them and felt she had made a good choice.

Unfortunately, the couple decided that they did not want to move forward – and my daughter was devastated. I realized that my daughter's reaction was much the same as mine twenty years before, when that one teenager we had met changed her mind and decided to parent. It was very difficult to watch my daughter go through this challenging experience, but we grew closer as a result. She and I had several intimate middle-of-the-night conversations during the pregnancy.

For several weeks, Marielle could not bring herself to look at other prospective couples. Finally, she went through her packet of profiles again and with her boyfriend's help, chose another couple that lived locally. They talked on the phone, and then made plans to have lunch together. Everything went well and my daughter and her boyfriend were matched again.

Marielle's due date was still four weeks away, but she was showing some symptoms of pre-eclampsia, a serious condition that can occur during pregnancy and cause complications for the mother and the baby. Her doctor sent Marielle to the hospital for what ultimately ended up being induced labor. Over the next five days, I camped out in her hospital room. My husband and Marielle's boyfriend joined us once the induction process had begun.

Our daughter invited the adoptive parents to the hospital to discuss plans for the delivery, as well as to meet Mark and me. When the adoptive mom walked into the room, she and I instinctively looked at each other and then hugged as if we were long-lost relatives.

Immediately after the baby was born, my husband, my daughter's boyfriend and I stayed in the delivery room for about an hour. As the birthgrandmother, I treasured having some time with my precious grandchild. Then Marielle's boyfriend went out to the waiting room and invited the adoptive parents to come into the room and meet their son.

I felt like I was in some sort of weird time warp. I sent text message announcements to family and friends, including Marielle's birthmother, who had now joined me in becoming a grandmother. After an hour with all of us together, the nurses had to send my daughter to the post-partum unit. They gave the new adoptive family a room next to hers, so she could see the baby during her recovery period.

One of the hardest things I have ever had to do was leave the hospital the next day without my grandson. I felt so much like crying but managed to put on a strong face. If my daughter was not going to cry, then I wouldn't allow myself to cry either.

Fortunately, the adoptive family lives locally and we have had several visits with them. Marielle also visits on her own and tries to include her ex-boyfriend, although they broke up several months after the birth. We can see that our grandson is one lucky little boy to have so many people who love him dearly.

We Will Teach Him Your Name

by Erin Garcia-Norris—Adoptive Mother

I am writing our son's birth story on the eve of Mother's Day. It is the third year in which my wife Rory and I can celebrate the day as moms to Ari Mariano Garcia-Norris.

Every Independent Adoption Center adoption story I read gives me an emotional tug as events unfold for these families in such unpredictable, yet meant-to-be, ways. It is in looking back that we can make sense of all the seemingly unrelated events that have led us to be parents.

Our first encounter with IAC was seeing their booth at the San Francisco Pride Parade. I already knew at that time that I wanted to raise a child, but adopting was not a part of my plan. Rory and I laugh now when we remember our first reaction to open adoption; "What? A birthmother will be a part of making our family and may even be considered family?"

Now we complain because Ari's birthmother, Eunice, lives far from us; we only hear from her occasionally via email and phone calls. We really wish that we were closer to each other so that she could regularly experience what an amazing child her baby has become.

We received only two birthmother contacts before our match. The first came only three weeks after we finished all the paperwork, including our birthparent letter and online profile. That birthmother chose someone else; she decided she was looking for a single person to adopt her baby. We went into waiting mode again.

We had just met the one-year mark and were scheduled to meet with our counselor about going on the Last Minute Hospital List. Then we received a call from the IAC; there was a birthmother in Los Angeles who was six months pregnant, and she wanted to talk to us. The counselor told us she did not speak English, only Spanish. She asked if Rory, whose last name is Garcia, spoke Spanish. But Rory, who is Filipina, does not speak Spanish.

I speak enough Spanish to get by on a vacation in Spain, but talking on the phone about pregnancy and adoption seemed too challenging. But this was a chance to become parents, so we enlisted our Spanish-speaking friend Marvin as our interpreter. I took a half-day off from work and we called the birthmother, Eunice, at the scheduled time.

During the conversation Marvin interpreted and calmly told us, "And you already know it's a boy, right?" Although gender was not important to us, we started shouting, "It's a boy! It's a boy!" It was very exciting to learn something about our prospective child; suddenly our dream seemed closer to reality. For Eunice, our enthusiastic reaction was one of the first positive moments she had experienced during her pregnancy. She could not believe that people she hadn't even met were so excited about it.

We flew to Los Angeles to meet Eunice. There was some miscommunication as to where to meet her, but we finally figured out that she was on a bus headed to her medical clinic for an appointment. I worried that maybe there were some complications with the pregnancy; otherwise why would she have planned to meet us on the same day she had an appointment?

We arrived at the clinic before her and wondered if we were on a wild goose chase. We did not know what this mysterious birthmother looked like. There were two or three clinics on the same street. All around us were pregnant women speaking Spanish. We felt ridiculous looking at each pregnant woman and wondering … "Are you carrying my child?"

We overheard two women speaking in Spanish. Did they say "Eunice?" It is an uncommon Hispanic name; was that her? The receptionist told us that Eunice had already had her appointment and had left. Then "our" Eunice called my cell phone to say that she had just stepped off the bus. We went back outside on the busy boulevard and there she was, crossing the street.

We had imagined that meeting a birthmother would be awkward. How do you talk to a stranger about such intimate details of life? How do you balance the absolute joy the adoptive parents feel with the sadness and loss the birthmother must be feeling?

We went to the clinic with Eunice and sat in the waiting room while she had a routine appointment. To my relief there were no complications, but we did learn later that when the nurse found out that Eunice was considering adoption, she tried to talk her out of it.

After the appointment, we finally talked and showed her photos we had brought. Before we knew it, Eunice asked us, "So, what do you think?" My instant response was "We love you."

We had planned to take her to dinner and then give her the weekend to think about matching with us. As we were driving to dinner, a translator connected with IAC called. During this conversation, we discovered that Eunice had no place to go that night. Apparently, everything she owned was in the little bag she was carrying.

After discussing how to find her a place to stay, we discovered that she was willing to come live with us. We cancelled our return flight reservations and began driving the rental car back to Northern California.

We had just three months to get to know each other. We would never have believed it could work if it had not happened to us. We were able to provide Eunice with healthy meals, take her to her prenatal appointments, and give her reasons to laugh.

I had initially thought adoption was all about the child, but it deeply touches all those involved. Our "translator friend" Marvin is now Ari's beloved *tío*. My parents are grandparents for the second time and our brothers are uncles. Eunice is our dear friend who made our amazing dreams of creating a family come true.

Eunice felt sadness and loss, but because she chose open adoption, she can also share in the joy that she made possible. On Ari's adoption finalization day, Eunice called us to share her happiness with us. She said, "I made a conscious decision to choose the best for my baby. You taught me that love is also respect, smiles, hugs and patience. Ari will know how to be loved and to love, how to respect and be respected. You have changed my way of thinking about the world, you opened my mind deeply." (Eunice also honed her English skills while living with us.)

At two years and five months old, Ari continues to amaze us as he learns and grows. His list of accomplishments already includes reciting the names of all 44 presidents, enjoying listening to us read chapter books aloud and completing the U.S. state puzzle unaided. Recently he said, "I want to talk to birthmother Eunice" when he heard that she was on the phone. Just as he knows that he has two devoted moms raising him, he knows he also has a birthmother who chose this loving family for him.

In an email on Mother's Day last year, Eunice wrote, "This day could look like one of those sad days, but it is not. Being a mother is a different and unique experience, the most pure expression of love. With this in mind, I feel that I'm a mother. When you're a mother everything is possible. There are no borders, languages, or colors, only the need to give love and have the courage to give it in a conscious, responsible way. Thank you for every hug, for every night and day I was with you and thanks for teaching Ari my name. You're the most beautiful mothers that I know."

Eunice, we were honored to teach Ari your name. There was never any doubt about it.

Editor's Note: When Ari was four years old, he became a big brother when Erin and Rory adopted their second son.

Finding Declan's Little Brother

Part I: Bringing an Adopted Child into a Family with a Biological Child

by Julie Roberts Sanders – Adoptive Mother and Biological Mother

We wanted our story to be that of a couple who, unsuccessful in getting pregnant, turned to adoption and within a few months were parenting a newborn … totally unprepared and amazed at how quickly their life turned around. Or the story of a couple that magically got pregnant after finally taking their focus off infertility.

Our first pregnancy was deceptively easy, but my husband Jay and I endured years of painful waiting for a second child. After four years of trying we had an obsessive relationship with the calendar and the odd kind of sex you have when you're just trying to hit the fertility window. We knew too well the thrill of being "late" and the shattered hopes of another unsuccessful cycle.

We finally chose to give up and embrace our life as a one-child family. We knew our son Declan was a blessing. We tried to live in acceptance, but nagging feelings remained.

We researched other options and decided to pursue open adoption. Although initially cautious about the "open" part, we loved that the birthmother would choose her baby's parents and truly believed that would be healthiest for all involved. We knew the wonders of the early months, so we were excited about having a child from birth. We had let go of being pregnant, but we did not want to let go of having a newborn.

After choosing open adoption, we wanted to do it right. We worried and wondered about the process ad nauseam. How should we word our letter so that a birthparent would choose us? What photos would catch a prospective birthmother's attention? How long do adoptive parents typically wait? Can we afford this? How can we avoid frauds? How can we protect our hearts? More important, how can we protect the heart of our 5½-year old son? Waiting for a match, or just a call from a possible birthparent, was the hardest part of the process. Among adoptive parents, it seems that one partner tends to be calm and Zen-like, while the other (that would be me) crazily tries to control everything. When I looked at the amazing couples waiting along with us, it was hard to remember that we were not *competing* for a baby. Then a friend who had adopted twice reminded me that it just takes one contact – the one who chooses you.

Fortunately for me, adoptive parents no longer have to create a physical scrapbook about themselves that an agency can show to a birthparent. Now you create an online profile that can be accessed from anywhere in the world. If you add a hit counter, you can check to see if someone visited your profile; sometimes you can even tell where that person lives.

You can imagine the stories I made up while studying the hit counter. "Someone in Philadelphia looked at our site twice today. Stay by the phone, I'm sure she'll call us any moment." Or, "someone Googled 'Scooby-Doo' and ended up at our site. Could that mean we have a deep connection that could only result in an adoption?" "Oh no, no hits today. I am devastated and cannot go to work." Eventually I learned that you never really know what it means. I had to just wait and wonder.

Fortunately, I discovered an equally-obsessed friend-in-waiting at the IAC's Adoption Information Seminar. After signing up we emailed or called a few times every week, cheering each other on when contacts were made and soothing each other when the journey seemed impossible. Our partners were relieved that we had found each other. It freed them from having to talk constantly about the process that had engulfed our lives.

Three months went by. Our hope of an early match and a dream story began to fade. Discouragement set in; we wanted a baby, but there was nothing we could do to quicken events. We just had to wait. The IAC suggests you network during this time, which is like getting the nursery ready when you are pregnant. It keeps you focused on something you can control while you are on an out-of-control ride.

Our first real contact came after four months of waiting. We were on vacation, and my husband received the call while we were walking home from the beach. We were nervous and excited. The prospective birthmother was friendly, and we talked for well over an hour. It felt more comfortable than we had anticipated.

The birthfather said they would contact us if they were interested in moving forward; we never heard anything more. Did they choose to parent? Did they choose someone else? It was invigorating to get our feet wet, but it was difficult not knowing why this road had come to a dead-end.

Seven months into the process, my husband spoke with a prospective birthmother for nearly 30 minutes. He felt positively about the call, and I was supposed to phone her that evening. I tried, but there was no answer. My heart sank as I added another disappointment to the pile.

Surprisingly, she called back a few days later. I talked to her for more than an hour, sitting on a bench with a Halloween carnival and soccer games going on behind me. She told me about herself, her children, and the baby she was carrying; she had me laughing a lot. She said I had a wonderful husband and that she wanted to choose us.

We felt exhilarated. We were ready to call our friends and family with the news and fly to North Carolina to meet her as soon as possible. Then, the IAC counselor called and asked, "What did she tell you?" Her emphasis on "you" told me that it was not good news. She had spoken to other couples and the birthmother's story was not consistent, which indicated that this was probably not a real situation. It was even possible that the "birthmother" may not have been pregnant.

We were embarrassed that we let her exploit our vulnerability and felt ashamed for committing our emotions so easily. It became hard not to view the hit counters as proof of enemies peering at our profile and trying to hurt us, rather than as the reminders of hope that they had been before.

In early November, we received an email from another prospective birthmother, Eliza. She asked us to answer sixteen thoughtful questions and added that we were doing an amazing thing, even if she did not choose us. It felt so positive that I burst into tears.

Jay and I stayed up until 1:30 a.m., answering the questions and remembering why we loved each other. We hit "reply," and then we waited. One week later she actually called us. "I've narrowed it down to four couples," she said. "Can we meet in person?" The day after Thanksgiving we had our first birthparent meeting. The prospective birthparents were in their mid-thirties, unmarried and with no other children. It was better than we could have imagined and we all hit it off.

On the way home, Jay and I decided we really wanted to parent their child and hoped that they would choose us. Nine days later she asked to meet us again. We shared another dinner, talking until the restaurant closed. Could it feel any better than this?

Our IAC counselor called a few days later to tell us that the birthmother had narrowed her choices down to two couples, and we were one of them. She wanted a week to think, and then she would contact us with her decision. It felt like living a television cliffhanger.

I received the call at work. "Eliza has chosen to match with you and Jay," said our counselor. I cried with glee and frustration. Eliza was just three months pregnant and we would have to wait another six months for our dream to come true.

Those six months felt like a dance of open adoption. We spent time with Eliza so that she would get to know us and feel confident about the family who would raise her child. In addition, we gave her space, so she could go through whatever she needed to go through in order to make this huge decision. We included Declan, our son, in the relationship, but we did not tell him right away that we might adopt Eliza's baby. We wanted him to feel free to be himself and to not feel responsible if it didn't work out.

There were many unexpected obstacles during this period. Eliza's mom frequently tried to change her mind and every new doctor would question her decision. Outsiders would tell her how wonderful it is to be a parent and friends often came up with new options to consider. When you are pregnant and contemplating adoption, everyone has something to say, even if no one talks openly about it.

As the weeks passed, the controller in me began to let go. Although I really wanted to be the mommy of this baby, I also realized the magnitude of the decision for the birthparents. Walking alongside Eliza, I felt great compassion for all prospective birthmothers. All along, I knew we could not be certain what would happen until the actual birth. Even when all the ducks are in a row, the relationships strong all around, the decision seemingly made, the baby items purchased and ready ... no mother knows what it feels like to say goodbye to her newborn unless she has actually done it. As a mom, I could not imagine it, even if it was clearly the most loving decision. I admired the courage and selflessness of anyone who could.

Three days before her due date, Eliza and her mom stayed at our house because it seemed labor was imminent. They slept in our bed while Jay and I were in our son's bunk bed. No one slept soundly, knowing that our lives were about to change forever.

About 6 a.m., Eliza, her mom, her boyfriend and Jay and I headed to the hospital and spent the next 16 hours in the labor and delivery ward without much action. Eliza's mom chatted non-stop. We watched TV (including a preview for a show about adoption scams!); we took turns taking walks, doing errands for Eliza, contacting family and friends.

When the anesthesiologist arrived, Eliza was an evangelist, telling him about the wonders of open adoption. Around 11 p.m. her labor finally kicked in. Jay camped out in the waiting room, but I was fortunate enough to be in the room to experience the miracle of birth. At 12:32 a.m. on June 16, the long-awaited, healthy boy was born. But in that instant, some part of me knew that he was not going to be our baby.

It would have been easier if the realization had been as clear to Eliza as it was to me. Jay thought I was being neurotic, so I tried to ignore my feelings. The next three days were surreal and perhaps the most painful of our entire adoption journey. Eliza went through the motions, even having the baby discharged with the name we planned to give him, but I could tell her heart was not in it.

We did not know what to do or say. We had never been in this situation before; maybe this was a normal part of adoption. Ironically, Eliza's mom was the most enthusiastic and kept talking to Declan about his new brother. Jay and I were concerned about Declan bonding with the baby.

After leaving the hospital, Eliza and the baby spent a night at our house. Not willing to do that again, we pressed her to make a decision. Tearfully, Eliza just said, "I didn't know." When a baby is theoretical, you can make plans in your head. When he is in your arms, your heart gets very involved. All along, Jay and I told each other we would be thrilled to parent Eliza's baby if she was not able to do it. She had simply discovered that she *was* able.

I felt numb during the two months that followed. Helping Declan deal with the disappointment increased our heartbreak and sense of guilt. By choosing open adoption, we had caused him to deal with loss and complex emotions at a young age. However, since he had five months of friendship with Eliza before finding out about the possible adoption, his lack of an agenda seemed to make him more resilient and understanding. He said, "Well, somebody was going to hurt. I guess this time it was going to be us." Fortunately, having a baby in our house for just one night made all three of us certain that our baby was out there somewhere.

A few weeks later, we visited Eliza, her boyfriend and the baby. Although we still felt the sting of the process, in some strange way we had helped make a family. As we looked around their apartment filled with new baby things, we knew that this part of our journey was over. It was a relief to let go and move on.

In early August, we entered back into the world of waiting with a new-and-improved letter and online profile. On August 30, we received an email from another prospective birthmother, who was due in just six weeks. Her profile was not ideal, especially because she did not discover she was pregnant until 24 weeks along. However, we were open to this new situation. We knew that we could survive six weeks of anything!

Her emails were straightforward, but sporadic. It was hard to be patient between contacts, but we already knew that letting go of our timing and agenda was an important part of the process. Her emails felt honest and encouraged our questions. At one point, she asked if we were seriously considering adopting her baby. If we were not, she wanted to find someone else.

She seemed committed to simply placing the baby; she was not interested in an ongoing relationship. Her main goals were to choose her child's parents and to have a "mommy" in the delivery room to greet the baby. She felt it would be harder to let go if she was the first to hold him.

After four weeks of only email contact, we set up a lunch date. We were trying to hold things lightly, but were quite disappointed when she cancelled just prior, saying she was not feeling well. We were relieved when she contacted us later that weekend; we met for dinner on Sunday.

Mandy was 30 years old and the single mother of two boys. Her boys meant everything to her, but she knew that she could not adequately provide emotionally or financially for another child. She had not planned to get pregnant again and would have terminated the pregnancy if she had known sooner.

Interestingly, she liked us because of Declan. She wanted her baby to have a brother, the way her boys had each other. She was refreshingly open, no-nonsense and had a wonderful laugh. Having given birth before, she seemed to have an emotional understanding of the choice she was about to make.

When we left the restaurant, she handed me a hospital pamphlet and an ultrasound picture. I gladly looked at them and handed them back to her. She said, "No, these are for you. This is your baby." Those words touched me deeply, for Mandy had already treated us more as the parents-in-waiting than Eliza ever had.

Two weeks before Mandy's due date, we had our match meeting. We told our story, including our disappointment with Eliza, and she shared more of hers. Ironically, a couple she matched with prior to us had "disappeared." So, we all had felt abandoned in the adoption process before, which made our commitment to each other even stronger.

Mandy had been hiding her pregnancy from her boys and had planned to keep it that way. After speaking with our adoption counselor at the IAC, she understood the benefits of including her boys in the process. After the meeting, she told her older son about her adoption plan and was pleased by his acceptance. I think that gave her even more peace.

Just after 4:30 a.m. on Saturday morning, our toll-free number rang. "Hi, it's Mandy. I am in labor. It's time to come to the hospital." My sister quickly drove over to stay with Declan. We kissed him goodbye, believing his brother was about to be born. We raced off to the hospital with our hopes high, yet knowing the hardest part was still to come. It was raining lightly, and somehow that felt appropriate.

Mandy's mom and I were by her side through her relatively quick labor, and at 9:26 a.m. on October 14, Brody Roberts Sanders was born. We all cried - out of joy for us and out of sorrow for Mandy. I held him first, which was such an honor. He was peaceful and beautiful.

The bond between our families grew stronger during the hospital stay. Mandy's boys met Declan; they loved goofing around together and accepted each other easily. Mandy's mom, who had initially resisted the adoption choice, sent us a note afterwards about how she now understood the amazing love that goes into adoption. She was proud of her daughter's courageous and unconditionally loving choice, and she was relieved that she would still get to know Brody, the little miracle boy.

Leaving the hospital was hard on all of us. It had felt nice to live in a safe little bubble in which our two families could exist together. The reality of taking home the baby we had longed for, while leaving Mandy with empty arms, was bittersweet. How could we feel so overjoyed for ourselves and so deeply saddened for her at the same time?

I said to Mandy, "You are our angel." Mandy answered, "You are mine, too." With tears that come from a deeper place than words can express, we hugged and said "goodbye." It sounded like an ending, but it was just the beginning.

Having Brody makes this the best story we could ever tell. Riding the rollercoaster of love and loss, of letting go and being open, changed our hearts and lives and made our years of waiting meaningful. We are glad we did not become magically pregnant or adopt Eliza's baby. The story that led us to our Brody transformed our lives.

Over the next sixteen months, we visited with Mandy and her family four times. I emailed updates every month and sent pictures, too. For our first shared Mother's Day, we had a picnic together and Mandy gave us a beautiful book of adoption stories and photos.

Brody is now 6½-years old, and we continue to have a very positive, ongoing relationship with Mandy and her family. As another Mother's Day approached, I asked Brody if he would like to give Mandy a gift and he happily exclaimed, "Yes." Then, he proceeded to explain that while I am his real mom, she is his mom too, because she carried him inside her body.

Before living in an open adoption, I thought a comment like that might feel threatening, but it was not. On the contrary, I was thrilled. We want Brody to live without shame or secrets, knowing his miraculous story and experiencing the deep love of his birth and adoptive families. While decorating Mandy's Mother's Day card, Brody drew a picture, which seems to say he is getting that message. *(You will find the picture in the photo gallery.)*

Part II: Having a Brother Makes Me Happy

An Interview with Declan Roberts Sanders – Brody's Big Brother

When Julie & Jay Sanders began the open adoption process their son, Declan, was in kindergarten. Brody was born when Declan was almost 7½ years old and in second grade. At one point, the Sanders family, including young Declan, thought they had a match but the birthmother changed her mind after the child was born and decided to parent. We asked Declan, as a thoughtful big brother, to share his thoughts about his kid brother and open adoption.

What do you think it means to adopt a child?

To adopt a child means to get a child that the birth family cannot have because they already have more children or they cannot handle one. You get to have a baby and keep him.

What is your first memory of adoption?

We had to take many pictures, and it was so stressful. We took them over and over, and my mom and dad got mad at me. The very first picture came out the best. Then, we had to write a lot of letters, and I got 5 cents for each one I signed.

How did you feel about the fact that your mom and dad wanted to adopt a baby?

It felt nice that I was going to have a brother and that I'd have more company. It was sort of hard because it was my first time doing it. I didn't really know what my parents were doing and why they were doing it.

Did you want to have a brother or sister?

Yes, I did because it is nice to have company around the house…some of the time. I had it best because I was an only child for seven years and had my parents to myself. Now, I get to have a baby brother. So, I had to get used to my parents, and now I'm getting used to my brother.

What did you like about adoption?

I liked meeting new friendly people who worked for adoption and two nice birth families. Eliza had a fun personality, and she liked the Cincinnati Reds, just like me. Zachary and Zander (Mandy's boys) are nice, fun kids, and I like having them as brothers, too. I really liked holding Brody for the first time, and I liked the 'big brother' gift that he gave me.

What was hard about adoption?

My hand really hurt when I signed all the letters…again and again. I did not know what my parents were doing some of the time. And, it was hard not getting the first baby.

How did you get through not keeping the first baby?

When they told me, I hid in my bed. I didn't want to hear it. I just kept telling myself that "it's life, it's life, it's life" and "some bad things happen in life." My parents helped me by telling me that it wasn't my fault and Eliza said she still loved me. It was sort of stressful going back to school because I didn't want to tell everyone, so my dad told my teacher, and she told the class for me. My teacher cried and hugged me. The summer was kind of hard. I didn't want to be away from my mom.

How did you feel when your parents matched with another birthmother?

I kept telling myself "halleluiah." I hoped we were going to find the real Brody.

How do you feel about it now that you have your brother, Brody?

Having a brother makes me happy. I love him because he is enthusiastic and loving. It is fun how he learns bit after bit after bit. He thinks I am the best in the whole universe, and I can always count on him to laugh at me. Sometimes he's annoying, but I always want to have him and I don't want to change that in all of my life.

What was surprising about having a baby?

When he first came home, he didn't do very much but sleep. It is surprising how much he grows and grows. It was tougher than I thought…the crying, the schedule, the biting and stuff.

Were you ever nervous about not getting to keep Brody?

Yes, I was sort of scared at first because I wasn't sure what would happen. But when I met the birth family I wasn't nervous any more.

What is finalization?

I always think of "finally"… like, you've been through so much and now you finally, really have your baby. Brody got to know us, and then he got to have us. We could finally prove that he was ours.

What was it like to be at Brody's finalization hearing at the court?

It was weird how short it was. It was really fun. It was more emotional than I expected.

Is there anything else you would like to share?

We made a slideshow about our adoption, and we used the U2 song "Oh, Can't You See What Love Has Done (Window in the Skies)." I like that song because it really shows what our love has done to our future and our family.

Three Weeks to Zoe: A Surprise Journey to Joy

by Ruth and Christopher Traylor – Adoptive Parents

A year after we were married, Ruth became pregnant with a little girl. She miscarried at six months due to complications from her lupus. The doctors told us that we had a very low chance of a successful pregnancy.

Ruth was adopted, so we had always talked about adoption as an option to build our family. The Independent Adoption Center seemed to be just the agency we were looking for. IAC appeared to be an open agency with a wide variety of couples and single adults that had adopted or were waiting to adopt a child.

We attended the information seminar and signed up for the next adoption workshop. We made it through our home study, then took a couple hundred photos in order to get two we liked for our birthmother letter. We then started on the text. Who knew it would be so difficult to write about yourself? We went through thirty or more drafts of our letter, and just about gave up. Finally, after Labor Day, we had an approved birthmother letter.

Just five days later, we received a call from the North Carolina office of the IAC. A birthmother who received our letter in the mail that morning wanted to contact us. She was due in just three weeks, and we received a call from her that evening. We completely forgot about the list of questions we had made, but we hit it off right away, and the conversation flowed easily.

After speaking with the IAC counselor again, we booked flights to

North Carolina for a match meeting. But on the day of our flight, we received another call from the IAC. Our birthmother had gone into labor a week early and was going to deliver later that evening. We raced home from work, packed a few clothes for ourselves, and what seemed like a million items for the baby. When we checked in at the airport with an empty car seat, the airline employees kept asking where the baby was. We told them we were in labor and on our way to the hospital. That earned us some odd looks!

We did not make it to the delivery, arriving a few hours after our daughter, Zoe Nicole, was born. When we walked into her birthmother's hospital room, she started crying and we started crying, and she said, "Do you want to hold your daughter?" The answer was, "Of course."

We spent two days at the hospital with our daughter and her birthmother. We spent the time getting to know each other. Among other things, she told us she was a drummer, just like Chris.

Our official match meeting happened the day the hospital discharged Zoe. After we discussed our plans to remain in contact, Zoe's birthmother had chosen to sign the relinquishment papers. We left the room. It took almost an hour for her to sign the papers. We were extremely worried that she was going to change her mind and she later told us that she almost did.

We took Zoe back to our hotel room on that Friday afternoon. We were prepared to live in the hotel for another two weeks, but on Monday, we learned that the Interstate Compact for the Placement of Children had approved the adoption paperwork in record time. We would be able to go home by Wednesday.

We had planned to meet Zoe's birthmother for lunch on Tuesday. We waited in the car for her to drive up to the restaurant. To our surprise, she arrived with Zoe's birthfather, who we had not met before. We became nervous that they wanted to take Zoe back. We almost drove off, but decided to stay.

Instead of having lunch, we talked for a few moments at an outside table. We told the birthfather that we would do a good job raising Zoe, and that we hoped her birthparents would still be a part of her life. He told us that he could tell we were good people, and the fact that he would be able to see her again made him comfortable with the adoption.

We also told the birthparents that we would be going home to California the next day. They understood that we wanted to get home, and that Zoe had excited grandparents waiting to meet her. We took pictures together for Zoe's scrapbook and her birthmother gave us a letter to read once we were home in California.

We flew home to California on the first flight out on Wednesday morning. Our parents embraced their new granddaughter immediately. Later that evening, after everyone had left our house, we sat down as a new family and read the letter from Zoe's birthmother. The letter explained why she had placed Zoe for adoption and that she would always love her. She went on to say that we were the parents that Zoe was meant to have.

Everyday we are amazed at how wonderful it is to be parents and how much fun Zoe is. Adopting her has been a life-changing experience for us. It took just three weeks from the time our birthparent letter was approved, to taking our new daughter home. We know this may not be the norm, but we would not have had it any other way.

Coming Out on the Other Side

by Tiffany Ward – Adoptive & Biological Mother

My husband and I had a long and sometimes painful journey to becoming a family. One thing that always held true was our faith that someday we would be on the other side of our efforts, where everything would be as it was supposed to be.

We spent many years together before marriage, so when we married we planned to start a family right away. It took us just four months to conceive, and like most first-time parents we anxiously awaited our ultrasound. After the exam we learned that our baby had very significant heart and kidney defects; we chose to terminate the pregnancy. The doctor told us that the baby's defects were just an unhappy coincidence and that we could try for another baby in a couple of months.

We endured many months of waiting and experienced two additional miscarriages while trying to conceive again. Our fertility doctor then told us that I had a great deal of scar tissue that would require surgery before we could try for another pregnancy.

We were delighted to discover that I was pregnant just weeks before my scheduled surgery date. But our delight turned to devastation when we learned that our baby boy had a kidney condition that would require intrauterine surgery to correct. We consulted a perinatologist and a surgeon and learned that, once again, we would not deliver a healthy infant.

We chose to deliver the baby in the hospital to learn all that we could from an autopsy. The geneticists discovered that my husband and I had a very rare recessive gene that causes Fraser Syndrome, which results in severe birth defects in 25% of pregnancies. We were heartbroken, but also relieved to have an answer.

We knew the odds of having a healthy pregnancy would eventually turn in our favor, but how many more tragic pregnancies could we endure? I began exploring adoption and found it was the best way to build the family of two to three children that we yearned for.

I discovered the Independent Adoption Center after doing some research on different methods of adoption. We attended the information seminar in October and just two weeks later we joined the agency. I jumped into the big job of filling out the paperwork, which we finished in mid-December.

Just one week later we received an email from our birthmother entitled "My Baby." We will never forget it. She was eight months pregnant; we met her and her 12-year old son one week later. We were scared and nervous, but as soon as we met them, we felt at ease. As they drove away after the meeting, we knew that our world was about to change quickly and in the most amazing way.

Our son, Everett Hollis Ward, was born in February. We were ecstatic, overjoyed and then overwhelmed when we left the hospital with our baby that we had waited so long for. Three nights later, I looked at my husband and said, "So he lives here now? He's just going to stay and be our baby?" I felt sheer bliss now that I could cry for joy rather than pain.

Everett was an amazing baby; he ate well, slept well, and lit up our whole world with his squinty-eyed, gummy smiles. People are still in awe of Everett's sweet smile and sunny nature. Almost every day he throws his head back in laughter, just like his momma, as he claps his hands with zeal.

Our relationship with Everett's birthmother and her son continues to be a warm and comfortable relationship to this day. We met her parents just before Everett's birth and were happy to make an easy connection with them as well. We are excited that Everett has many people in his life to love him.

Shortly after Everett's birth, we learned that I was pregnant again and that the baby was healthy. We were going to have two babies less than seven months apart and we felt so blessed.

My pregnancy was smooth and sweet, and we delivered our second son, Hudson Graham Ward, in September. He was beautiful and wise and most important, very healthy. We look at Everett and Hudson today and know that this was how it was supposed to be. The boys wrestle, and snuggle, and fight and giggle together every day, as if they were always meant to be brothers.

We adore our sons and we are grateful that we are where we knew we would be one day, on the other side.

Editor's Note: Tiffany had two more successful pregnancies, and the Ward family welcomed two additional sons to their family. She and her husband are now the busy parents of four active boys.

Over the Rainbow –
Our Journey to Multiculturalism

by Lane Mashal –Adoptive Father & Former IAC Counselor

My husband Steven and I were married in 1997 at our San Francisco synagogue. Soon afterward, we began exploring avenues for adoption. Like many Independent Adoption Center families, we investigated county adoption, international adoption, surrogacy, attorneys, and agencies. We were initially most interested in county adoption, as the need was greatest there. However, we decided to go through an agency so we could adopt an infant, which is rarely an option with a county agency.

We found out about the IAC at a meeting of Maybe Baby, a support group for LGBT prospective parents. There we met another gay male couple that had just adopted a baby girl through the IAC. We knew right away that IAC was everything we wanted in an agency. It was the only agency that treated us as equals with heterosexual potential adoptive parents. We wanted openness and loved the warmth and support they offered to birthparents and adoptive families. We had noted that many agencies and attorneys were not respectful of birthparents, speaking of them in a patronizing manner and referring to them as if they were mere vessels for adoptive parents. We wanted an agency that understood birthparents' difficult choices and used counseling to foster an open relationship between all parties.

After signing up, we averaged one contact a month, but no matches resulted. Then, at one of our many support groups, we met a Caucasian family who had adopted an African American baby. Right in front of us was this happy family, and we saw how it could be for us.

We had submitted our original profile as "Caucasian only." Steven was more fearful than I about handling the challenges involved with transracial adoption. He used to say to me, "Will our black child want to bring his black friends home to meet his two white Jewish daddies?"

We began asking African American women and men, often strangers, what they would think if we adopted an African American child. We wanted to know if the African American community would accept our child and we received mostly supportive responses.

Then we presented our plans to my parents. They were worried about the discrimination that their grandchild might encounter due to anti-Semitism, homophobia, and racism, but offered their full support. However, they still worried – as did we.

We started to get contacts from black women and were surprised that some actually liked us *because* we were Jewish. Many asked what we knew about raising black children in our society. We responded that it would be a learning experience, but we understood the support that our child would need from educators, peers, and role models. We also pointed out that Steven and I had spent our lives in two minority groups and knew what it is like to encounter discrimination, ignorance, and hatred.

Our first match was with an African American birthmother from the Bronx. She had four boys and her husband had died shortly after she became pregnant. Unfortunately, she decided to parent when she gave birth to a girl. We tearfully returned the winter clothes we had bought in preparation for a trip to the East coast.

Then one day, while I was working as a special education teacher's aide, the school office paged me. An IAC counselor, Colby, was on the phone; she asked, "Do you want a baby?" I said "yes," my heart racing. Colby said we should come to the hospital in an hour and pick up our baby boy. The birthmother did not want to meet us, but Colby said she would try to convince her otherwise.

When we arrived at the hospital, the baby's birthmother agreed to meet us. As the hospital planned to discharge her shortly, we were only able to talk for thirty minutes. She told us that she had named the baby Jonathan Israel - the same names we had picked out in the car on the way to the hospital! We chose to use the name Yonatan, the Hebrew/biblical version of Jonathan. To this day we get goose-bumps from that memory.

Our son's birthmother was African American and the unknown birthfather was Hispanic. Unfortunately, we never had contact with

Yonatan's birthmother again. We began our journey as a multiracial family with no connection to our son's birth family or heritage.

We pondered what our predominantly white neighborhood would be like for a child who stood out. The only other people of color in our community were nannies. While we encountered nothing negative in our time living there, Yoni (the Hebrew diminutive for Yonatan) was the only child of color -- and we were the only gay parents.

We decided to find a more diverse community and moved to a different neighborhood a few miles away. There the schools are like little United Nations communities where they celebrate each ethnicity and no one is an oddity. Our child would have African American and Hispanic peers and adult role models. We liked that the children made friends and had play-dates, and the adults were friends as well.

Our choices have been essential to our child's development. He feels that he is just one part of a diverse world rather than the only representative of an alien culture.

When we were ready for a second child, we wanted to ensure he or she would be of an ethnicity different from ours. That way Yoni would not be the sole sibling who did not look like his daddies. Ironically, our second adoption profile read "open to any ethnicity, except full Caucasian."

We received several calls from birthparents of various ethnicities who were interested in us because we were already raising a biracial child. They too wanted their child to be raised in a diverse and tolerant environment.

We adopted Shai, a boy whose birthmother, grandmother and great-grandmother lived 20 minutes from us. We see them frequently, usually once every month or two. Shai will always know them, and they have the joy of watching him grow. They have truly become part of our extended family.

Shai's extended birth family has also been a benefit for Yoni, who has found it difficult to understand why his birthmother has not been in contact with us. Fortunately, the connection with Shai's birth family gives Yoni a tie to his heritage and the chance to know a birthmother whose story was similar to his own birthmother's. She was 19, with no high school diploma, living with her grandmother. She wanted a better life for Yoni and she wanted to be able to finish school.

Shai's arrival led to some interesting new experiences. His features are more "typically" African American, and people who had previously seen Yoni as "mixed" or "biracial" now saw him as African American. To this day, people often comment that "they could have been biological brothers."

We always marvel at this, since our sons have distinctly different features. Is it that white people cannot see the physical differences between persons of color? Or do others think that adoptive parents prefer to hear this because it would be rude to say that the children do not look like each other or like us?

Although we have found that there is no one place to live, nor group to join, that can satisfy all the needs of our children, we have tried to give them guidance and options that can help them build self-esteem and a healthy identity. We have joined many organizations including PACT (a multiracial adoption group), the Jewish Multiracial Network (who knew?) and the South Bay Adoption Group. We also belong to South Bay Families Together and PopLuck Club, which are specifically for families with gay parents.

Our children go to religious school at our synagogue to embrace our Jewish religion and culture. If only my mother were still alive to see her African American/Hispanic grandson reciting the Sabbath prayers and singing in the synagogue choir. And who could have predicted that our son's Christian birthmother, grandmother, and great-grandmother would be guests at our annual Passover seder? This is just part of the richness that diversity has brought to our lives and the lives of those around us.

Editor's Note: The IAC hired Lane as an adoption coordinator when Shai was about one year old. Lane was instrumental in developing the agency's online transracial adoption training. He now works on a contract basis for the agency while being a stay-at-home father to his two sons.

Adoptive Mother, Birthmother, Best Friends

by Amanda Sgro – Adoptive Mom

When our beautiful daughter Eden turned five, I found myself reflecting on our adoption journey. It seemed like yesterday that the doctors told my husband John and me that we would not be able to conceive. We decided to pursue an open adoption through the Independent Adoption Center.

About two weeks after completing all of the requirements, we received a brief email from a potential birthmother. Bre was a high school senior who was facing some hard decisions and was looking carefully at all of her options.

Over the next seven months, Bre and I became the best of friends. We would spend hours online late at night, chatting. We talked about everything from our fears and hopes for the baby, to how our days were going, and who had said something stupid or insensitive that had made us mad.

When the time came, John and I headed down to Bre's home town, arriving the night before the big event. We had dinner at the home of Bre's parents. (For the record, Bre's mom makes the best burgers ever.) The next morning, the call came; Bre's labor had begun.

It was time to head to the hospital. After what seemed like forever, Eden made her appearance. We were overwhelmed by a range of emotions - pure joy and excitement about our new daughter, and sorrow and despair over the pain that we knew Bre would soon be facing.

Bre was one of my best friends; almost like a little sister. How could I watch her face that? We spent time everyday in the room with Eden and Bre. We met Bre's friends and family, including Aaron, who would later become her husband. Bre had a great support system.

We honored Bre's decision to have some private time with Eden each day, and tried to be mindful of her needs in that very difficult time. As it came time to sign the papers and leave the hospital, emotions were high. We all shed many tears. I had no words of comfort to give my friend. All I could do was reassure her that our relationship was not over; that she would always be welcome in our home and in Eden's life. Bre and her family have always been wonderful to us. We are lucky to consider all of them our family.

After leaving the hospital, we took Eden to our hotel. She was so tiny. We changed her clothes, fed her, and snuggled with her. We had planned to hold an entrustment ceremony later that evening. We took Eden to Bre's house a few hours before the ceremony so she could spend a little quiet time with her. She got Eden ready for the ceremony and brought her to the church. One of the most emotional parts of the service was hearing Bre's dad say how proud he was of her. I do not know many women that could have handled the situation with as much class and dignity as she did.

Years have gone by and Bre and I are still as close as ever. We see each other and talk quite often. When Bre married Aaron, we attended the wedding. John is a minister, and he performed part of the ceremony. Eden was the flower girl and I was a bridesmaid. We were so happy to be able to share in another one of the most important days of Bre's life. We felt fortunate not only for the gift of our daughter, but for her birthmother and her entire family.

Who Will Pick Me?

by Gretchen Long – Single Adoptive Mother

I always pictured that I would have a family sometime between the ages of 30 and 35. When 35 came up on the calendar and there was no special person with whom to share my life, let alone start a family, I began to explore my options.

Being a mom and having children in my life is simply who I am. I have always known that, just as I have always known my name. It is why I chose to become a teacher, and why I chose open adoption.

I attended an information seminar at the Independent Adoption Center's Los Angeles office. I came away certain that open adoption was a perfect fit. Of course, I also had a mile-long list of questions, which were really fears and concerns. In particular, I had major worries about why any birthparent would ever pick a single woman.

I think it was easier for me to choose adoption because as a single person, I only had to consider myself. Although my family and special friends had their concerns, they were all supportive of my choice to adopt. So armed with my list of questions, I attended the adoption workshop in July and took the next step in becoming a family.

By the end of November, I had completed all my paperwork, the home study, and my online profile. I matched the following May and my beautiful son Jack was born in September.

As I prepared to meet my son's birthparents for the first time, I felt so nervous I did not know how I would make it to the meeting, let alone through the meeting. I had so many fears and worries; would they like me, would I have anything to talk about with them, would I be able to be myself so that they could get to know me?

I agreed to meet them at a restaurant an hour's drive away. I knew I could not survive the drive on my own, so I talked my mom into going with me and waiting in a coffee shop until I was done. I brought three photo albums with me (something someone had suggested at the orientation) and was so grateful that I did. The albums helped break the ice, gave me something to talk about while I calmed down, and helped them get to know more about me.

We ordered food, which I barely ate, and talked for more than an hour. I was surprised at how comfortable I felt with them. I had to lead the conversation quite a bit because they were young (16 and 17 years old) and very nervous. I admitted how nervous I was and that I had made my mom come with me. They ended up wanting to meet her after learning how close we were. It was an incredible first meeting.

They called me on my way home and told me that they wanted to move forward with me. My heart was overjoyed and the rollercoaster ride was underway.

Looking back, I am in awe of how everything worked out for me. I am so grateful for the amazing gift of having Jack in my life. I will always feel love and gratitude for Jack's birthparents and hold them dear to my heart. I hope his birthparents will always be in our lives, and will go on to do wonderful things in their own lives.

I have a long list of hopes for the future, like all parents. At the top of the list is that Jack grows up healthy and happy, knowing many people truly love him. I also hope to find my Mr. Right and give Jack a bigger, fuller family life, perhaps with a sibling or two.

Three Points of View
Part I: Dreams Do Come True

by Elizabeth Lasher – Adoptive Mom

Our first two years as a family have been fantastic! Our son Kyle is a very happy, affectionate, and healthy little boy. Our visit with his birthparents last summer was the highlight of the year.

As Kyle's birthday approaches, I remember where my husband Mark and I were just three years ago. We were anxious for the phone to ring and nervous each time we spoke with a potential birthmother. When we didn't receive a call for days, we worried that we were not good enough. If we missed a call, we would wonder if we had missed our chance to be a family.

When there were no calls or visits to our online profile for two months, we were at the lowest point in our journey. Then a young woman from San Diego called. Moments later, our lowest low had turned to hope. As we grew to know Megan and Sam better, we felt our hope turn into happiness. While they were no longer together as a couple, they agreed on making an adoption plan for their unborn child. At our match meeting in Los Angeles, we dared to utter the name we had chosen for the child. His birthparents, Megan and Sam, loved the name Kyle right away.

The days following Kyle's birth felt surreal to me. I was there when Kyle was born and stayed with him in the neonatal ICU until he could be released to our room at the hospital. We took him to visit with Megan and her family, and Sam and his family spent time with us in our room. We said a tearful goodbye to Sam at the hospital, listening to him pour his heart out while he sang to Kyle the song his own mother sang to him as a child.

After the hospital discharged Megan, we had a very peaceful goodbye with her in her home. Then we started our long journey back to our home. It was not until we stepped over the threshold that we fully realized that our dream had come true. We were now a bona fide family of three!

In the short two years since, we have shared all of Kyle's milestones with his birth families. When we have not heard from them in a while, we wonder if they might want to have less contact with us and our hearts ache, for they are a part of our family. We remember that they are busy young people working hard to realize their dreams. Then, sure enough, the phone will ring or we will get an email with updates on what's new in their worlds and we will feel connected again.

We've far exceeded what we promised in our open adoption agreement. Every other year we travel to San Diego in the summer to visit Kyle's birthparents, and this past year we shared our Christmas holiday with them too. With every visit we learn more about Megan, Sam, their families and our beloved Kyle.

Kyle now knows his adoption story. When Megan came for a visit to his school, Kyle introduced her as his birthmother and shared pictures of his birth families with his classmates! Friends and acquaintances marvel at how invested we are in our relationships with Megan, Sam and their families. To us, it is just a sea of love that surrounds our child.

Two years ago we could not have imagined how blessed, rich and full our lives would become. We cannot imagine having adopted any other child, and are incredibly grateful to have such an "open" adoption. Whenever anyone says that Kyle is lucky to have us, I just smile and know that we are the lucky ones.

Part II: With All My Heart
by Megan Parry – Birthmother

When I was 19 years old I found myself dealing with an unplanned pregnancy. I was scared out of my mind. Getting pregnant was not in my plan. My plan was to finish college, get a good job, marry a nice boy, and then start a family. Of course, life does not always work according to plan.

The second I found out I was pregnant, I started considering my options. Abortion was the first one I crossed off the list; I did not think I could live with myself if I made that decision. My choices were between parenting the baby and adoption.

I knew in my heart that I couldn't give this baby the life he deserved, but is anything harder than giving up a part of you? After wrestling with the decision for months, I decided to get some information about adoption. Like any teenager, I went to the Internet.

In the middle of the night, sitting in front of the computer in my pajamas, I found the IAC. I knew the only way I could survive handing my baby to someone else to raise would be through open adoption. I wanted this little one to never have to question where he came from and to know the whole truth.

After getting in touch with a counselor from the IAC, I received a big box in the mail. It was filled with the profile letters of potential adoptive parents. I avoided that box for a while, but finally I sat down and began slowly working through the letters. Mark and Elizabeth were among my top three favorite families. We emailed back and forth and I talked to them on the phone. Just hearing their voices, I knew they were the right ones. The love and kindness they had for each other and for a baby they had yet to meet were overwhelming.

In January they came down to San Diego to meet me. I brought so many people along with me that I think I overwhelmed them a bit. They may have been nervous, but you could not tell from their smiles and kind words. They immediately put me at ease and confirmed my decision that they were the right parents for this child. In any pregnancy, there will be people with strong opinions about what you should do. It's no different with adoption. I remember vividly that not everyone thought I was making the right decision. But my family was incredibly supportive, as were the wonderful people at the IAC.

In the two years since Kyle was born, my belief in open adoption has continued to grow stronger. I keep in touch with Mark and Elizabeth through emails and phone calls. With open arms, they have welcomed my family and me into their own. My mom went to Kyle's baptism, and Mark and Elizabeth always manage to send pictures for every big event in his life. I'm not saying that every day is perfect. I still struggle with feelings of loss, but knowing Kyle is with amazing parents like Mark and Elizabeth calms my fears. I am so thankful that there are people like them in this world.

Thanks to Elizabeth and Mark, I look forward to having a relationship with Kyle when he gets older. I take great comfort in the fact that they are always aware of my feelings as Kyle's birthmother. Even though the decision to make an adoption plan was the hardest one I will ever make, I know with all my heart that it was the right one for Kyle and me.

* * *

Afterword

Since writing my story, I graduated from San Diego State University with a Master's in English and was hired as an adjunct instructor at Grossmont Community College in San Diego. Teaching had always been my dream, and I could not be happier in my professional life.

Even better news is that my relationship with Mark, Elizabeth, and Kyle has grown in ways I never could have imagined. I see them at least once a year and talk to them on a regular basis.

Kyle has grown into a sensitive, caring and enthusiastic boy. Seeing him in school and at home reinforces my belief that I made the right decision six years ago.

My role as "Birth-me Megan", as Kyle calls me, is one that he and I are happy with, and I'm so blessed to know that he'll never have to wonder about his birth story. People always say that my decision was a gift for Mark and Liz, but really, the gift is that I gained more family than I ever dreamed possible.

Part III: My Favorite Story to Tell
by Sam Cummings – Birthfather

When I begin to tell the most beautiful story of my life, something that holds so precious a spot in my heart, people are often surprised. "You have a son and you gave him up?" is the most common reaction. I just smile at their incredulity and continue telling the story; it is, after all, my favorite story to tell.

Becoming a dad was always on my bucket list. But becoming a college graduate, a Master of Science, a "Mr. Cummings" in my classroom, and a "Mr. Right" to the perfect girl were supposed to come first. I cannot describe the overwhelming fear I felt when I received the harsh reality check to my perfect little plan. What was I going to do? As much as I would have liked to think of myself as an adult, I was not sure I had grown up enough to be everything a baby would need me to be.

Megan and I sat and cried. Weighing our options took a toll on our minds, our emotions, and each other. The only things that remained strong were our love for our baby, and our wish for him to have the life he deserved. But we could not possibly give him that life, no matter how hard we tried.

The decision to choose an open adoption brought the first feeling of relief in a long while. I had known for a long time that I simply could not "give up" my son for adoption, and that placing him with a family was the only acceptable option. Some would argue that "giving the baby up" and "placing him" are the same thing. They cannot understand the peace that comes from choosing someone who will not replace you, but rather supplement your love in a more stable way.

Choosing to place our baby was actually easier than I had thought it would be. Yet when we started the process, I found myself trying to be logical, pulling back and weighing the pros and cons. I had built up in my mind that there was no way that Mark and Elizabeth were going to be right. After our first meeting, however, I had to fight the urge to tell them the good news they had been praying for, just in case it was too early to say it.

Subsequent meetings, and countless e-mails and phone calls, reinforced this feeling. My parents met Mark and Elizabeth for the first time just weeks before Kyle was born. After dinner, my mother cried and said, "You're giving these people a gift they deserve. These are great people and this gift is going to change their lives, and yours."

Since Kyle's birth, it has been nothing but a miracle that keeps on getting better. Sure, it hurts at times; it would not be life if it did not. There are days, sometimes weeks, when loneliness gets the best of me. Then my heart is restored by a simple picture, a happy memory, and the knowledge that my son is in a loving home with wonderful people who couldn't possibly be more prepared for the job of parenting.

Kyle has four parents and countless extended family who love him so much that the cup that is supposed to be either half empty or half full instead overflows. I call this 'wasteful love' because you have so much you do not know what to do with it.

I see Kyle occasionally, when I have time to sneak away from work and school to make the seven-hour drive to his home. I do not intend to let our closeness and openness fade. Wherever I go, I know that I will always be thankful for the open adoption experience I have had. I am proud to say that my son is getting so much love and support. I wish I could tell the world; it is, after all, my favorite story to tell.

Our Little Miracle

by Maura Montellano—Adoptive Mother

The Journey Begins

Although Katherine and I had tried to have a baby via insemination, we never felt that we had to have a biological child. We wanted to be parents and made the decision to adopt as naturally as we had made the decision to have a baby. We knew little about open adoption, and we held typical preconceived ideas about the process. Like many adoptive parents we feared that the birthmother would show up at our door one day demanding to see her child, or worse, wanting the baby back.

After researching agencies online, we attended the two-day adoption workshop at the Independent Adoption Center in May. The amount of information was overwhelming and the process daunting, but two days later our minds and hearts were made up.

We immediately tackled the birthparent letter, at times chafing at the constant editing requests from our counselor. It is surprising how difficult it is to summarize your life, and how challenging it is to write about yourself. On our website, we did our best to highlight all the things we felt a birthmother would be looking for. We hoped that our passion and all the love we had to give a baby would come through in our photos and our words.

We dreaded the home study, but ended up enjoying the process. The IAC approved us soon afterwards and we were "live" in March. We were proud of ourselves, and predicted that in short order a birthparent would choose us. We smile now at how confident we were then.

Our first contact came in late August, followed by at least a dozen more contacts over the next seven months. Some contacts ended after one call; others ended after many weeks of emails. Our hopes were always high and our excitement palpable. Inevitably, disappointment and heartbreak were part of the process. We grieved and comforted one another after two potential matches did not work out.

By the following March, Katherine and I had an honest discussion about how long we could continue the journey. We were emotionally weary and our confidence had dimmed. Thinking that perhaps adoption was not in the cards for us, we made the painful decision to set a deadline. The date we chose was July 24, my birthday.

The weeks passed without a single contact. Neither of us spoke of the looming deadline, but we prayed we would be matched in time. On June 20, out of the blue, Katherine said, "Someone's going to contact us soon. I can feel it."

One month before the deadline, we received this email:

Date: Tue, 22 Jun

Subject: Hello Katherine & Maura

To: msmaura

From: ashleigh

Hi, My name is Ashleigh. I am about to be 20 years old and I live in Southern California. I am about 3½ months pregnant and due December 19th. Im looking for a great couple to parent the baby im carring. 2 things id like to know before we exchange basic info is if your ok with matching up with a BM early in her pregnancy and if your talking to other BMs. Thank you for taking the time to read this email and I hope both of you have a great rest of the week. – Ash :)

I read Ashleigh's email in the car at a red light and screamed like a mad woman. I pulled over, my hands shaking, and forwarded the email to Katherine, marking it with numerous exclamation points! I quickly responded to Ashleigh and began our amazing journey with an incredible young woman.

We liked Ashleigh immediately. When we talked on the phone that night, we found her to be refreshingly honest and surprisingly uninhibited in telling us about her life. Katherine and I looked at one another in astonishment, amazed that she could tell her story without a hint of shame or fear of judgment.

She told us about her son, four and a half years old, who was her life and bliss. We learned that she was a recovering addict and had been sober for almost three years. She was proud of herself and her ability to straighten out her life, in spite of incredible odds. However, she was realistic about the commitment required to parent and she knew she could not care for another child at this stage in her life. The birthfather was no longer in the picture, and they knew they were not prepared to be parents.

We met Ashleigh a few days later, hoping we would be as comfortable with her in person as we had been during our phone conversations. We worried that she might not like us, or think we were too old.

The moment we hugged for the first time, we knew she was the one. Hours later, as we said goodbye, she said, "I'll call IAC on Monday, and let them know I want to match." Katherine and I hugged her long and tight.

On my birthday, at what would be the first of many doctor's appointments with Ashleigh, Katherine and I sat transfixed by 3D images of the baby on large screens before us.

Ashleigh later told us that our display of emotion touched her. She knew then that she had picked the right couple because, "you don't even know her and I can see how much you love her already." She wanted to feel that same joy surge through her the next time she was carrying a child, because then she would know it was the right time for her to parent.

Birth Day

We drove to the hospital in December in giddy anticipation, holding hands and saying, "Oh my gosh, it's really happening!" a lot. For months we had talked about the day when we would become parents and now it was here.

When we arrived, Ashleigh appeared a bit fatigued, but was not in any pain. We were grateful her mother was there with her. We settled in, not realizing the long wait ahead of us.

At four the next morning Ashleigh was still nowhere near

delivering. After spending an uncomfortable night on a narrow cot, Katherine and I got a room at a hotel across the street to get some rest and freshen up.

At about 10:30 a.m. Ashleigh texted us that she was 8 cm dilated. We rushed to her side, held her hands, and tried to comfort her. We watched a monitor, giving her a heads up when the next contraction was coming. Though the pain must have been intense, she was not screaming or writhing in agony as we had witnessed on shows like "16 & Pregnant" and "Birth Day."

We put on hospital gowns and caps, laughing at how silly we looked in our "HAZMAT suits." Our friend Rita recorded those moments on video as we prepared to follow Ashleigh into the delivery room.

Now everything seemed to be happening so fast. Nervous energy filled the room as nurses prepped Ashleigh and summoned the doctor. While I held Ashleigh's head and shoulders and Katherine held one of her legs, we kept count with the doctor and nurses as we all urged her to push.

In the six months we spent with Ashleigh, we only saw her cry once. Now, as she saw Katherine and me holding our daughter, crying out that she was perfect, she wept again. Later she told us, "They were tears of happiness at seeing the picture I had in my mind all this time come to life before my eyes." Her sentiment and courage moved us profoundly.

Finally Home

We brought our daughter Gia home on Christmas Eve, after a one-week hospital stay. We were thrilled that we would be waking up on Christmas Day with our little miracle. The change to our household was immediate as we began to adjust our routine to Gia's. We had never imagined that such extreme sleep deprivation existed. Slowly, though, we settled into a routine and actually started sleeping again. With the exception of a nasty bout of colic, Gia surprised us when she began sleeping through the night at five weeks.

Gia is everything we wished for and more. She is an energetic, curious little girl with a stunning smile, now displaying four teeth. She erupts in a squeal when she sees her mothers. I'm a budding photographer and she has become my most inspiring muse; I never tire of capturing her delightful moods.

On July 8, three years, one month and two weeks after beginning our journey, we stood before a judge who declared Gia our daughter forever. The excitement shared by our family and friends at Gia's Forever Day party the next day doubled our joy.

We shared the news with Ashleigh, as we have done since Gia's birth. She immediately commented on Facebook, "It seems like it was just yesterday I had emailed you guys... I couldn't imagine Gia with anyone else ... I'm so damn lucky God was on my side and put you both in my path. I don't think I'd feel so complete if it wasn't for both of you. Thank you guys. And I'll love you forever for this."

Although Ashleigh has chosen to not meet Gia until she asks to meet her birthmother, we have shared updates and photos on a weekly basis. Ashleigh cherishes the photos and proudly shows them off, boasting of our happiness, Gia's beauty, and above all, her own peace with her decision to place.

Ashleigh looks forward to meeting Gia one day and introducing her to her half-brother. Until then, we will share with our daughter the story of her courageous birthmother, her loving choice, and our incredible journey to becoming her parents.

Holding Chloe for the First Time

Interviews with: Dahlia Bagnis - Adoptive Mother and
Brittney Warner - Birthmother

Dahlia's Interview

What brought you to adoption and the Independent Adoption Center?

The first time Ken and I visited the IAC, we were not quite ready to take the step toward adoption. We finally joined after almost two years of infertility struggles, hopeful that we would finally build our family.

Adoption had always been something I had considered, but with so many options available, making a decision was daunting. The more I read, the more I felt certain that open adoption was the right fit for our family. We wanted our child to have as much information as possible about his or her birth family and, if possible, the opportunity to maintain a relationship with them. But as much as we wanted our child to have this gift, we were also ambivalent about welcoming strangers into our lives this way. Who would our child's birthparents be and would they be a good fit for our family?

We signed with the IAC in March and feverishly worked to complete our home study and birthparent letter. It was an arduous task, but quite fun at times, and helped us regain the sense of control that infertility had taken from our lives.

We were so positive about our decision to adopt and believed so firmly that we were meant to be parents that we expected to get the call as soon as our paperwork was completed. In May, we at last joined the ranks of the waiting IAC families, and then — nothing happened.

Days, weeks, and months went by without so much as a scam contact. I tested our email account and 800-number frequently, just to make sure they were actually working. I tracked the number of hits to our online profile. How could it be that not a single birthmother had contacted us? I began to feel rejected, as if we just were not good enough. Our wait for a birthparent contact brought every negative thought and painful emotion bubbling up. As friend after friend got pregnant, I felt that familiar feeling of loss of control creep back in.

Had I known I would be bringing home my baby girl just a couple weeks shy of the one-year mark after our paperwork was completed, I would have spent that year differently. I would have enjoyed a few good vacations, smiled and laughed with my friends, and decorated a nursery. Instead, I often felt hopeless and at times doubted our decision to adopt. That is the uncertainty of open adoption, and I'd venture to say that I am not alone in my experience.

During a particularly bad week in February, we received a call from the IAC informing us that a birthmother was interested in speaking with us. Her name was Brittney, she was 18 years old, and parenting a 16-month old son with her boyfriend, who was 20 years old. She was six months pregnant and they did not feel capable of parenting a second child.

Brittney lived in a little town outside of Las Vegas that we had never heard of. We were told she was nervous about calling, but would be contacting us within the week. There was hope, finally. We researched the town where they lived, which was just a four-and-a-half-hour drive from our home in California. We waited for the call.

What was your first conversation with Brittney like?

Brittney called the following week while I was in a meeting at work, so I missed her call. She left a sweet message saying that she was nervous to talk to us. It took me about an hour to work up the courage to call back. My boss had to order me into my office to return the call before I actually did it.

In hindsight, it is almost comical that I was scared to call. I am a licensed clinical social worker, and at the time I made my living talking to people about intimate subjects. I think I was worried that I would say the wrong thing, and that I would feel that sense of rejection yet again.

My first conversation with Brittney was amazing. I liked her immediately and we spent quite a bit of time giggling about how nervous we were. I wanted to get to know Brittney and for her to get to know me. I shared with her how Ken and I met through the Los Angeles music scene and gave her a window into our lives. She shared with me her dreams of finishing high school, attending college, and moving out of her hometown.

Days passed before I heard from Brittney again, but I felt certain that we had made a connection. She called again a week later and I had a chance to talk to the birthfather. I liked him right away too. He too was genuine in sharing his fears. Ken was also able to speak with the birthparents, and it quickly became apparent that we were building a relationship.

As the weeks passed and the relationship grew, Brittney's intake counselor suggested a face-to-face visit. Brittney agreed, and we made plans to visit her for a couple of days. I asked her for suggestions of places we could go, and she told me there was a bowling alley, and that was about it. We planned to meet in the bowling alley on a Saturday in March. Brittney sent me pictures of herself, her boyfriend, and their son Tyson, so I would recognize them when we met.

Driving to the meeting felt surreal. We were on our way to meet the potential birthparents of our daughter. Was this really happening? As reality sunk in, I started to worry again about rejection. Would they change their minds and stand us up? Would they like us in person? All of these questions rolled around in my head. My husband, the eternal optimist, assured me that if we could be ourselves, they would like us.

What was it like to meet Brittney, the birthfather, and Tyson for the first time?

We arrived at the bowling alley early and sat down to wait. My heart raced as I watched a young, pregnant woman and her boyfriend walk into the bowling alley. It was Brittney and the birthfather; they did not stand us up.

We greeted each other with hugs and laughed about how nervous we all were. To break the ice, Ken and I had brought along some gifts. Brittney was running low on maternity clothes, so I had picked out a few pieces for her, along with a small star necklace to symbolize following her dreams. For the birthfather, we brought a USC hat; it's my alma mater and his favorite football team. We brought a drum for Tyson, to represent our love of music.

The four of us spent that afternoon together, bowling, eating lunch, and talking. It all felt surprisingly easy and we seemed to hit it off. Brittney and the birthfather shared their reasons for choosing adoption and I was blown away by their maturity and love for their baby. They wanted her to have opportunities that they just were not able to provide. It was clear that their decision had been painstaking to make and they were willing to sacrifice so much to give their baby the life they dreamed of for her.

Before returning to Los Angeles the following morning, we met for breakfast. That's when we got to know their son, Tyson, a bright little boy just learning to walk and so interested in his surroundings. Brittney and the birthfather were loving and attentive with him and it was obvious that they were exceptional parents.

In the week that followed our visit, Brittney requested to officially match with us and we gratefully accepted. They were wonderful people that we felt honored to welcome into our lives. We brought all three of them out to Los Angeles for a long weekend for our match meeting and a little sightseeing. It was, of course, the rainiest weekend that I had ever seen in Los Angeles, but we still managed to have fun, visiting a local children's museum and the beach, sharing meals, and just hanging out.

By the time of our match meeting we all felt like we knew each other pretty well. The process of firming up our adoption plans no longer seemed daunting. I felt confident that we were all on the same page. Openness is something that Ken and I were completely in favor of, but it was important to us to honor what Brittney and the birthfather wanted. If they had not wanted regular contact, we would have respected that.

Brittney and the birthfather had voiced fear over how their daughter would respond to her adoption, and to them. We assured them that their baby girl would grow up knowing that her birthparents are amazing people and that they made their decision out of love. We ultimately agreed on regular telephone contact, sharing of photographs, and one to two visits each year, which we could build upon over time if it felt right.

How did it feel to match and what did you do during "the wait"?

There were some very difficult questions to answer during the match meeting. Who would name the baby? Who would be present for the birth? Who would be the first to hold the baby? Brittney again amazed me with her maturity and selflessness. She invited Ken and me to be present for the birth and asked that I be the first to hold the baby in the delivery room. She told me I was the baby's "mom" and I should have those experiences. I was overwhelmed. Me, a mom!

They were eager to know which names we had chosen. I had had my heart set on the name "Chloe" for years and Kenny and I had chosen "Star" as the middle name. Brittney and the birthfather were the only ones who knew this secret middle name until after Chloe was born. They loved the name and began using it when talking about the baby.

Ken and I were going to be parents in just two short months. I laugh when I say "two short months" because that time really felt like an eternity. As ecstatic as I was, I could not help but feel terrified at the same time. This baby that I could already picture bringing home belonged to Brittney and her boyfriend and they were making the hardest decision I could imagine. Who could fault them if they changed their minds?

Brittney and I texted daily and we visited every couple of weeks before Chloe's birth. Our relationship continued to grow and I felt more attached to Brittney. I never doubted her intentions, but some part of me still felt scared. I waited until April to start to decorate Chloe's nursery.

How did you prepare for the birth?

There was so much to do to prepare for Chloe's birth. Emotionally, Ken and I were more than ready to be parents. What we were not prepared for was the logistics. Brittney did not have a car, there was no public transportation available, and they lived one and a half hours away from the Las Vegas hospital where Brittney would deliver. How were we going to get to Nevada in time to get Brittney to the hospital when she went into labor? We ultimately decided to travel to Las Vegas before Brittney's due date and crossed our fingers that she would not go into labor early.

About two weeks before Brittney's due date, her doctor decided to induce her labor. With just a couple of days to plan, we booked vacation condominiums just off the Las Vegas Strip for the birthparents and ourselves. We thought it would be nice for Brittney to recover in comfort for a few days and looked forward to being able to spend time together after the birth. My parents also arranged to be there.

We picked up Brittney, the birthfather and Tyson on the morning of the induction. We dropped Tyson off at his grandmother's house and the four of us then traveled to Vegas. We had a big lunch, and my parents were able to meet the birthparents for the first time. Later that day, the hospital admitted Brittney.

Describe the hospital experience.

The hospital staff started the induction that evening and the four of us hung out in the delivery room until we could barely keep our eyes open. The nurses had not yet started administering Pitocin, the labor-inducing drug, so Ken and I decided to stay the night at our condo. The birthfather promised to call us if anything changed. I slept fitfully, with my cell phone next to the bed.

Ken and I went back to the hospital as soon as we got the word that Brittney was awake and ready for us to return. The nurses started the Pitocin that morning and Brittney, the birthfather, Ken and I made bets on when Chloe would be born. I guessed 4:00 p.m., Brittney guessed 4:30 p.m., the birthfather took 5:00 p.m., and Ken settled on 6:00 p.m.

Brittney won the pool. Chloe Star entered the world at 4:27 p.m. on May 7. She was perfect in every way; a healthy 6 lbs., 11 oz. and 19½ inches long, with a full head of strawberry blond hair. The nurses who helped deliver Chloe were amazing. One had adopted a baby several years ago and was supportive of our participation. She ushered Ken and me to the warming table and told us to bring our camera. They asked Ken if he wanted to cut the umbilical cord. His hands shaking, he bowed out and I quickly stepped up. I was not going to miss a thing.

The birthfather had stayed by Brittney's side throughout labor and delivery. We have a beautiful photo of them holding hands just minutes before Chloe was born.

What was it like to hold your daughter for the first time?

The nurse placed Chloe into my arms for the first time, and as I gazed at her it struck me how much I already loved her. She was just incredible, and so were her birthparents. Brittney asked to see Chloe and commented on how beautiful she was.

Chloe was born on Birthmother's Day, the Saturday before Mother's Day, and Brittney wished me a happy Mother's Day. I will never forget that moment.

The hospital released Chloe and Brittney the next afternoon. We all traveled back to the condo together where Brittney got some rest. Meanwhile, Ken and I began to build a routine with our daughter. Chloe ate and slept while Ken and I just stared at her. She was so beautiful and we were in complete awe that she was ours.

I guess there is something to be said for having a baby at a young age, because the next morning Brittney was up and ready to start the day. The time we spent together turned into a family vacation of sorts. We had meals as a group and spent as much time together as possible while caring for a newborn. Brittney, the birthfather, and Tyson even did a little sightseeing.

We continued to bond during these days, and talked more about the adoption than we ever had. Brittney shared that she and the birthfather had initially feared a fully-open adoption and had considered choosing a family that lived as far away from them as possible. Thankfully, something about our letter stood out, and I think the relationship we were able to build helped to calm some of their fears.

Brittney and the birthfather thanked us for making the adoption experience as easy as possible. They gave us gifts; a "Mom" necklace for me, a "#1 Dad" hat and t-shirt for Ken, and a picture frame for Chloe. This gesture floored me. They had already given us the most amazing gift we could imagine and were now thanking us. I cannot say enough about how amazing these two are.

We had gifts for them as well; a bracelet with a "C" inside of a star for Brittney, and dog tags for the birthfather with the same symbol and the date of Chloe's birth.

How did you say goodbye to Brittney, the birthfather and their son?

Driving Brittney, the birthfather, and Tyson back home a couple days later was painful. I was sad to say "goodbye," but also felt the pain they must be experiencing in saying "goodbye" to Chloe. Like our previous goodbyes however, it was really a "see you later." We had a picnic in the park a few days afterward as we were not yet cleared to leave Nevada with Chloe.

A little more than a week later, we finally received the clearances required by Nevada and California to take the baby across state lines. We were excited to bring Chloe home. It was difficult caring for a new baby in a Las Vegas vacation condo.

What is it like to be first-time parents?

It has been four months since our daughter was born and it has been the best four months of my life. Chloe is a bright and happy baby. I love watching her develop new skills and cuddling with her when she is not on the go. Maybe it is the painful experience of infertility, but even on the hardest days, parenting is nothing but a joy for me. I go to bed feeling fulfilled and wake up excited to see the smiles and squeals the day will bring.

I cannot fully put into words how grateful I am to Chloe's birthparents for trusting us to be her parents. I am finally a mom to the most lovable little girl in the world.

What are your thoughts on open adoption now that you have experienced the entire process?

We've just finished up our first visit with Brittney, the birthfather, and Tyson since we left Nevada. I continue to be amazed by the open adoption experience. When we started out, we expected to become parents, but did not realize that our family would grow to include the birthparents and their son. They will be able to watch Chloe grow up and will be able to tell her themselves just how much they love her. Their picture sits in her bedroom in the frame Brittney and the birthfather gave her, and I talk to her about them often.

Chloe will get to grow up knowing her birthparents and her brother. There will be no secrets or unanswered questions. It is an amazing gift to be able to give to my little star.

* * * * * * * * *

Brittney's Interview

Describe what brought you to adoption and the IAC.

I knew I was too young to have another baby. I had not finished school. I knew I could find Chloe an amazing family, people who could give her a life I could never give her. What brought me to the IAC was I wanted to choose the best agency, and when I saw the agency online, I loved it. I knew it was the best place to go.

Explain your process for choosing a family. What stood out about Ken & Dahlia?

Well, the agency had sent a box full of adoptive parent letters. We read and read, and then came across Ken and Dahlia. I just knew they were the ones. What stood out to me was how much they wanted to have a baby and how loving and caring they were. I also liked that they were close to their families and would spend holidays with them. When I was a kid, I never had my family around and I wanted Chloe to be able to spend time with her grandparents, aunts, uncles, and cousins and be able to treasure moments like that.

How did the first conversation with Ken & Dahlia go?

It was indescribable; it was amazing. I was so nervous that I had butterflies in my stomach. After we talked for a while I felt comfortable, they seemed so fun, and they sounded like such great people. In my heart, I knew they were going to become wonderful parents and they were the right match for us.

Did you ever have any doubts or fears during the match? What were they?

Honestly, I had no doubts. Ken and Dahlia were perfect. I knew they would make incredible parents.

What was it like to meet Ken & Dahlia for the first time?

It was so incredible; my heart was pumping. I was just so excited to meet the parents of Chloe. It was just so wonderful I cannot even put it in words.

Explain what kind of contact you had with Ken & Dahlia during your match.

We had a lot of contact with Ken and Dahlia. I was in a rough situation and did not have a phone, so they bought us one. I was able to keep in touch with doctors, family, and of course, them, so I could let them know how my appointments went.

How did you prepare for the birth?

I wanted Ken and Dahlia, as well as Dahlia's parents, to be there. Ken and Dahlia rented rooms for us to stay in after Chloe was born so we didn't have to part early. We would be able to spend more time with Chloe because we didn't know when we could see each other again after that.

Describe the hospital experience.

The hospital experience was great. It was amazing to have them see

Chloe born and to witness how amazing she was. It was just so incredible.

What was it like to hold Chloe for the first time?

It was hard to hold Chloe for the first time because I just wanted to hold her forever even though I knew that she had wonderful parents. I loved her and I felt that placing her for adoption was the right choice.

How did you say goodbye to Chloe, Ken & Dahlia?

The goodbye was hard because I loved them all so much. I just could not wait to see them again because they were all so great to be around.

How has your life changed after bringing Chloe into the world?

My life changed incredibly. I just feel great knowing that Chloe is with safe, loving, great people and I love to share that with friends and family.

What are your thoughts on open adoption now that you have experienced the entire process?

Open adoption was a great experience because I gave a family something that is so important to their lives. I cherish having been able to provide Ken and Dahlia with a daughter, while still being able to have a relationship with her.

Editor's Note: Several months after Chloe was born, Brittney found out that she was again pregnant. Since the birthparents had formed such a great relationship with Ken and Dahlia, they decided to place Chloe's little brother, Colin Sky, with them as well.

Now That Our Children Are Grown: The Legacy of Open Adoption

by Nora Bergman – Adoptive Mother

Every prospective college student struggles with the challenge of encapsulating his or her life in an essay for the school applications. When our son applied to medical school, he emphasized the fact that he grew up in a family that took a leap of faith and braved the new frontier of open adoption.

More than 20 years ago, we took our first tentative steps toward ending our infertility merry-go-round when we attended an informational meeting with Dr. Bruce Rappaport, the legendary founder of the Independent Adoption Center. The IAC was then in its infancy, revolutionizing adoption with the previously unthinkable idea that birthparents should choose the adoptive parents and, if mutually agreeable, enjoy ongoing contact with their child.

We became convinced that open adoption was the only way to proceed. Our family and friends wished the best for us, but were also wary of the untested road we had chosen. Looking back, this period of time was fraught with uncertainty, anxiety and, at times, near-hysteria, but also with excitement because we were working to make our dreams come true.

As it turns out, our apprehensions were unwarranted. My husband Al commented recently to our son's birth family, "Can you believe we've known these lovely people over *twenty* years?"

We were blessed to adopt two babies, now 22 and 16, from different birthparents and ethnicities. Our son, Christian, is Chinese and our daughter, Sarah, is Hispanic/Dutch/German/Welsh. Although formed unconventionally, our family is like many others. We went through the same stages: bewilderment while nurturing helpless, miraculous babies; hovering over and protecting toddlers; the first tearful days at preschool; our children's assertions of independence; the teenage challenges of driving, dating and applying to college.

A foundation of openness and honesty has guided us. Our children knew and could tell their adoption stories from the time that they could talk. Both grew up with innumerable birth family pictures, letters, visits, and gatherings. (Christian more so than Sarah, as sadly we lost contact with her birthmother when she moved out of state years ago.)

Open adoption is an integral part of our lives. It established identities, answered the questions, and provided other significant connections and relationships for our children. The gifts of open adoption are other adults providing unconditional love and soft places to land for our children, who in turn feel empowered to try, fail, regroup, try again and ultimately flourish. Our children's birth families have had the peace of mind that comes from seeing the children mature and being able to play important roles in their development.

Whenever we get together, we feel like one big extended family - catching up with one another over delicious food and raucous laughter. We have the pleasure of trading kids' stories and exchanging parental tactics, discussing politics and world events, debating over the next "American Idol," reminiscing over the latest "Glee" episodes, singing karaoke together, watching dueling piano recitals, and much more.

Our families have grown close because we grew up together - with just seven years separating the youngest and oldest child. We lived through the same family stages and helped each other through life experiences with love, humor, and support.

Christian's birth family – June (birthmother), Joanna and Simon (aunt and uncle), Ramona (grandmother), David (grandfather) and Andrew and Phillip (cousins) all provide vital connections, sage advice and sustenance. For our children, they are beacons of light, who help them navigate through life, and we like to think we are the same to them.

Today, who would not opt for *more* people who care about their children? As Dr. Bruce Rappaport said, "It's a win-win for everybody." Even though Bruce has passed, the legacy he created with the IAC lives on forever in the thousands of beautiful families he helped create through open adoption.

Glossary

ADOPTION ATTORNEY – A lawyer or attorney whose practice specializes in conducting adoptive placements. Even if the placement is done through an agency, the services of an adoption attorney are used during the finalization of the adoption.

ADOPTIVE PARENTS – The couple or individual who become(s) the legal parent(s) of a child through the adoption process, which includes the termination of the birthparents' parental rights.

BIRTHPARENTS – The biological mother and father of the baby or child who is placed for adoption.

CLOSED ADOPTION – An adoption in which there is minimal, if any, identifying information exchanged between adoptive parents and birthparent(s). Typically there is no ongoing contact after placement. Historically, all adoptions were closed and adoption records were sealed.

COUNSELOR – The counselors are the clinical staff of an adoption agency who generally have a master's of social work (MSW) or similar degree. At the Independent Adoption Center, the **adoption coordinator** works with prospective adoptive parents during the wait and after placement. The **open adoption counselor** provides counseling and support to the birthparents and adoptive parents during the match. **Intake counselors** typically have a bachelor's degree and are the first point of contact for the birthparents.

DEAR BIRTHPARENT LETTER – Prospective adoptive parents compile text and photos into a "letter" that is provided to potential birthparents as an initial step in deciding with whom to match.

HOME STUDY – The process of preparing and screening prospective adoptive parents, including the completion of criminal background checks, physical exams, interviews and a home inspection, as well as additional forms. The home study must be conducted by a licensed adoption agency according to state regulations.

IN VITRO FERTILIZATION – A medical procedure that involves extracting eggs from a woman's ovaries and fertilizing them with sperm in a Petri dish, then transferring the growing embryos back into the woman's uterus. Infertile couples often try this procedure in an effort to achieve a pregnancy.

LICENSED AGENCY – An organization that is staffed by counselors with a master's degree in social work (M.S.W.) or similar degree. It is licensed by the state to place children into adoptive homes.

MATCH – When birthparents and adoptive parents agree to work together to plan the placement of the baby before birth, it is commonly referred to as "being matched" or "in a match."

OPEN ADOPTION – An adoption in which there is ongoing contact through letters, email, phone calls, photo sharing and visits after the baby is placed with the adoptive parent(s). The birthparents and adoptive parents typically meet prior to the baby being placed.

THE WAIT – The period of time between completion of the preliminary steps (i.e., Dear Birthparent Letter and home study) and the match between the prospective adoptive parents and birthparents.

About the Editors

Guylaine Hubbard-Brosmer, Ph.D., M.S.W.

Guylaine Hubbard-Brosmer is the national research director, home study supervisor and an adoption coordinator at the Los Angeles branch of the Independent Adoption Center (IAC). She has held other positions during her tenure at the IAC where she has been on staff since 2005. She has worked with hundreds of families during their adoption process and supervises a large, successful independent home study program. In addition, she has given numerous talks at conferences about agency adoption, open adoption and trans-racial adoption.

Dr. Hubbard-Brosmer has dedicated her career to family-building. She worked in the infertility field for 15 years following the completion of her Ph.D. in endocrinology from University of California at Berkeley. A career change led her to earn a M.S.W. from California State University Long Beach, where her thesis project was A Study of Trans-racial Adoptive Parenting and the Needs of Multicultural Families.

Ann Wrixon, M.S.W., M.B.A

Ann Wrixon is the executive director of the Independent Adoption Center (IAC). She succeeded IAC founder, Dr. Bruce Rappaport, when he retired in August 2006. During her tenure, the IAC has more than doubled the number of families for whom it provides services. IAC is a licensed adoption agency in California, Texas, Indiana, Georgia, North Carolina, Florida, New York and Connecticut.

Ms. Wrixon has spent her career managing non-profit organizations dedicated to improving education and child welfare. She has published widely on those subjects as well as adoption-related topics including open adoption, LGBT adoption, interstate adoption, and much more. Ms. Wrixon has a B.A. from Rutgers University, a M.B.A. from San Francisco State University and a M.S.W. from California State University East Bay.

True Stories of Open Adoption:

Family Photo Gallery

family photos from
How Openness Changed Everything

Top: Thom Kwiatkowski, and Ann Wrixon with their daughter Elizabeth
Bottom: Ann Wrixon

family photos from
My Life is All About Open Adoption

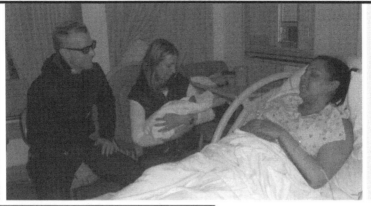

Top, Middle: Marielle, the adoptive parents with baby Ronin shortly after delivery
Bottom Left: After 20 years the visits with birth family are still going! (Back Row, L to R) Marielle, Mark, Guylaine & Geremy; (Front Row, L to R) Birthmother Stacey with Jack, Kelsey & Henry **Bottom Right:** Guylaine Hubbard-Brosmer

family photos from
We Will Teach Him Your Name

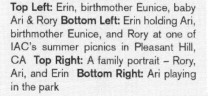

Top Left: Erin, birthmother Eunice, baby Ari & Rory **Bottom Left:** Erin holding Ari, birthmother Eunice, and Rory at one of IAC's summer picnics in Pleasant Hill, CA **Top Right:** A family portrait – Rory, Ari, and Erin **Bottom Right:** Ari playing in the park

family photos from
Finding Declan's Little Brother

Top Left: The Sanders Family **Top Right:** Brody & Declan smile for the camera! **Bottom Left:** A special Mother's Day doodle drawn by Brody (Age 6) **Bottom Right:** Julie & Birthmother Mandy with Brody

family photos from
Three Weeks to Zoe: A Surprise Journey to Joy

Top: Zoe is all smiles! **Middle:** Ruth, Zoe and Chris **Bottom:** A happy baby Zoe

family photo from
Coming Out On the Other Side

Above: Tiffany and Daniel with sons (L to R) Bo, Everett, Hudson, and Oliver

TRUE STORIES OF OPEN ADOPTION

family photos from
Over the Rainbow - Our Journey to Multiculturalism

Top: The Mashal family **Middle:** Shai's birth family with the Mashal family **Bottom:** The Mashal family with Shai's birthmother, Lexi

family photos from
Adoptive Mother, Birthmother, Best Friends

Top: Bre and Amanda **Middle:** Bre, Aaron, Eden, John, & Amanda enjoying the day together **Bottom:** Birthmother Bre on her wedding day with Eden

family photos from
Who Will Pick Me?

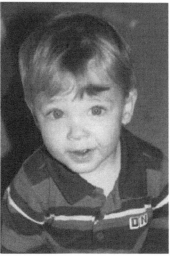

Top, Middle: Gretchen with her son, Jack **Bottom Left:** Grandmother, Mommy, & Jack enjoying the day together **Bottom Right:** Jack having fun at playtime!

family photos from
Three Points of View

Top Left: A family portrait – Elizabeth, Mark, & Kyle **Bottom Left:** Mark & Elizabeth with Kyle, and behind them the Parry Family: Grandfather John, Birthmother Megan, Aunt Brianne, and Grandmother Debbie at the Lashers home **Top Right:** Kyle shares a kiss with his birthmother, Megan **Bottom Right:** Sam, Kyle's birthfather, and Kyle spending time together

family photos from
Our Little Miracle

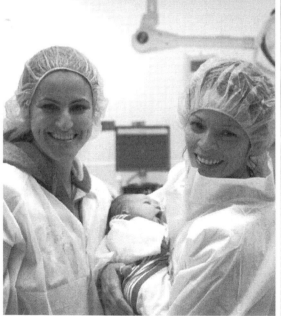

Top, Middle: With birthmother Ashleigh at our baby shower **Bottom Left:** Happy as can be, moments after Gia's birth **Bottom Right:** Gia enjoying playtime at the park

family photos from
Holding Chloe for the First Time

Top Left: Chloe being admired by her parents **Top Right:** Ken sharing a story with daughter, Chloe **Bottom:** Birthmother Brittany, adoptive mom Dahlia, and baby Chloe enjoying a walk in the park

family photos from
Now That Our Children are Grown: The Legacy of Open Adoption

Top, Middle: The Bergman family (L) at dinner with Christian's extended birthfamily (R) **Bottom Left:** Sarah & Christian with the family dogs, Foxy & Bella **Bottom Right:** Christian and June, his birthmother, in 2003

Made in the USA
San Bernardino, CA
16 December 2013